City Foxes

PHOTOGRAPHY BY WENDY SHATTIL
STORY BY SUSAN J. TWEIT

Denver Museum of Natural History & Alaska Northwest Books™

To Grandma Tillie with love and to Bob for his genius and generosity.

My gratitude extends to Ann Douden, for adoring my fox family and putting her heart in this book; to Susan Tweit, whose thousand well-chosen words convey the story in my photos; I thank Jamie Alton for his presence throughout and Heidi Lumberg for her guidance in the stretch.

—W. S.

For Marlene, who never lost her sense of wonder.

Thanks to Wendy for seeing the foxes; to Ann and Betsy Armstrong for seeing a book in the photos; to Ellen, Jamie, Annie, and Heidi for bringing the book to life!

—S. J. T.

Photographs copyright © 1997 by Wendy Shattil/Bob Rozinski
Text copyright © 1997 by Susan J. Tweit

City Foxes is supported in part by Valerie Gates.

Library of Congress Cataloging-in-Publication Data
Shattil, Wendy.
    City foxes / photography by Wendy Shattil; story by Susan J. Tweit.
       p.   cm.
    Summary: Records the lives of two adult foxes and their litter of newborn kits which have
    made their home in a city graveyard.
       ISBN 0-88240-493-8
       1. Red fox—Juvenile literature.   2. Urban animals—Juvenile literature.   [1. Foxes
    2. Urban animals.]   I. Tweit, Susan.   II. Title.
    QL 737.C22T88   1997   97-12756
    599.775--dc21   CIP
                                         AC

Originating Editor: Marlene Blessing
Managing Editor: Ellen Harkins Wheat
Designers: Ann W. Douden, Gail Kohler Opsahl

The photograph on page 24 has been digitally altered.

Copublished by:
Denver Museum of Natural History Press
2001 Colorado Boulevard, Denver, CO 80205-5798
303-370-6444

Alaska Northwest Books™
An imprint of Graphic Arts Center Publishing Company
Catalogs and book orders: P.O. Box 10306, Portland, OR 97210
800-452-3032

Printed on acid-free paper in Canada

One cold March night...

six baby red foxes were born in the midst of a busy city. Their home was a den dug by their parents, a grayish father fox and a rust-red mother fox, in the lawn at one edge of a cemetery. The young foxes—called kits—were born helpless and with their eyes shut tight.

At first the kits simply nursed and slept. But after their eyes opened, they began to explore the den on wobbly legs. Soon they were playing, nibbling on each other or on their parents, and tumbling over one another.

One afternoon in early April when the kits were sleeping, the mother fox slipped out of the den. She had been inside with the babies for too long. The father stayed behind, snoozing and watching the kits. The mother stretched out in the sun next to the den entrance and began to clean her fur. Lick, lick, lick went her tongue.

Like baby red foxes everywhere, the city fox kits spend all of their time in the den for the first month of their life. When their father isn't out hunting, the parents trade off baby-sitting.

In the den, a baby fox woke, hungry. The kit searched around—no mother. The kit whined. Its mother answered from outside. The baby walked up the tunnel toward the sound, but stopped, blinded by the bright sun. The den was familiar. The world outside was not. Its mother called again. The kit paused. Its belly growled. Finally, the fox kit trotted to its mother, flopped down, and began to nurse.

Soon three more babies woke. One by one, each
ventured out into the strange new world to find its meal.
The mother fox lay on her side, nursing. Just then,
a car drove toward the den on a nearby lane. Up went the
mother fox's head. Her big ears swiveled. The car slowed as its driver
spotted the foxes. The mother barked once. The four babies leapt up
and ran into the den hole with their mother close behind them.

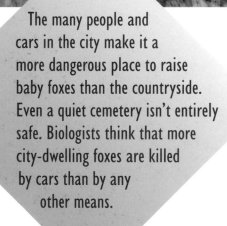

The many people and cars in the city make it a more dangerous place to raise baby foxes than the countryside. Even a quiet cemetery isn't entirely safe. Biologists think that more city-dwelling foxes are killed by cars than by any other means.

Foxes roll on the ground to bathe, then lick their fur clean. Working dirt into their fur helps scrub their skin and removes parasites, tiny animals that feed on their skin flakes.

The next afternoon, the mother fox came out to sun again. A baby fox followed her, yawned, and rolled in the grass. Then another appeared, and another, and another, and another, and another. Soon all six kits were out tumbling and rolling.

Although adult red foxes are nocturnal, the kits, like human babies, are up at all hours. They often come out of the den during the day to play. Fox parents everywhere hunt from evening through early morning. City foxes hunt in the daytime more, since city predators are less active then.

The mother sniffed the air, looked around, and listened. Sensing no danger, she yawned, showing her sharp teeth, and lay down to watch over her kits.

The following morning, a spring snowstorm hit. It snowed all day and through the night. The wet snow toppled trees, closed streets, and kept people at home. The city was quiet.

The fox family huddled together in the den, their thick fur keeping them warm in the freezing air. The babies slept in a pile, tiny black noses tucked beneath their fluffy tails. Every few hours, they woke to nurse. The mother and father fox napped, getting up now and then to peer out at the snow. They couldn't hunt until the storm stopped. It might be several days before they had food.

Four days later, the storm passed. The snow melted and the weather warmed. That night, the mother and father fox moved the family to a new den under a big tree, next to a row of gravestones. One by one, each parent picked up a kit by the scruff of its neck and trotted off to the new den. After they placed one kit in its new home, they went back for another. When all the kits were moved, the father went out hunting.

City foxes have to be especially careful, because cities are home to other predators, as well as pet dogs and cats. Pets hunt just as wild animals do when they are allowed to roam free. Red foxes move their kits to fool predators—other hunters. Animals such as rattlesnakes, coyotes, and great horned owls will eat the fox kits if they smell them and find the den.

Life at the new den was the same as at the old one: The young foxes slept, nursed, and grew. They played on the quiet lawns, safe from busy traffic and other dangers of city life. They sunned themselves on the gravestones.

Then, two weeks after the snowstorm, when the kits were about six weeks old, life changed. The fox family split up. The father fox took five kits back to the original den at the edge of the cemetery. The mother and one kit stayed in the den next to a gravestone.

What happened? Red fox families normally stay together until the kits are about five months old and ready to live on their own. The city foxes parted at weaning time, when the mother stopped nursing the kits. Foxes are weaned when they are between one and two months old. Perhaps the family broke up because one of the kits was not ready to be weaned. Maybe the father took the five weaned kits and the mother stayed with one that needed more care.

The father fox now had five growing kits to feed and care for by himself. He hunted day and night. The wild, brushy edges of the cemetery were good hunting grounds.

Whenever he returned to the den, one or more kits would run to greet him, reaching up to nibble on his muzzle. That nibble meant "Feed me!" The father fox grew thin. One ear was torn. Raising five fox kits was not easy.

The kits, small and wobbly when they first left the den, were now big enough to really play. And they played! A kit darted over and pounced on one of its sleeping siblings, biting the sibling's tail. The second kit woke up with a yip—"Ow!"—and snapped at the first. The two chased each other round and round until they collapsed, tongues hanging out.

Another kit grabbed the remains of a squirrel their father had brought and ran off with it, head held high. The rest of the kits chased the first, trying to grab the food. Then it was tug-of-war. Each kit grabbed a piece of the food and pulled as hard as it could. They growled and tugged, and growled and tugged, until the carcass fell apart and they all fell over backward.

Two kits started a play-fight, standing up on their hind legs and "boxing" with their front paws. They put their ears back, growled, and looked mean, with their pink mouths open and their sharp baby teeth showing. Later, the two curled up together and fell asleep.

As they play, the fox kits learn how to behave and how to survive. The kits grow stronger and more agile each time they chase one another. When they stalk and pounce on each other, they are practicing hunting. Sniffing each other and play-fighting teaches the foxes how to tell who is friend and who is foe.

By June, the foxes were over two months old. They wandered farther and farther from the den. They were curious about everything. Once, their father brought home a dead mallard duck, a new kind of food. The kits approached it cautiously, sniffing loudly. It smelled funny. They ran away. Their father lay nearby, watching the kits with his lips curved as if he were smiling. The kits ran up to him, begging for food. He turned his back. Finally, hunger overcame fear. The kits tore the duck apart and ate it.

Curiosity is important for foxes. They are omnivorous—they eat almost anything. They hunt anything small that moves, from mice to birds, and insects to earthworms. They also eat fruit like berries and cherries, and corn, and whatever else smells good. Being curious helps them discover new foods.

The father fox prowled farther and farther to feed his growing youngsters, often taking one or more kits with him.

There are more kinds of
food in cities than in the
countryside. City food could be
a stale pizza from a trash can, or
an animal just killed on the road.
Or pet food in a bowl left outside,
squirrels caught in a park, or
tomatoes from a pot on
a patio.

No matter
where they live, red
fox kits leave their parents
and their den at the end of their
first summer. They roam until they find
a place of their own. But city foxes have it
harder. Most don't survive their first year.
Life in cities is full of dangers for foxes—
traffic, pets, city-dwelling coyotes,
people. Outside of protected
spots like the cemetery,
safe places to live
are rare.

By mid-August, both fox dens were empty. Gnawed
bones and dried fox scat were scattered around the entrances,
but the dens were silent. The foxes were gone.

What happened to the fox family? Did the kits survive?

That fall, a beautiful red fox that looked just like the mother reappeared in the cemetery, sunning on the gravestone next to the second den. The following spring, that red fox and a different male raised a new family in the old den.

We don't know what happened to the kits in our story. Perhaps they survived, perhaps not. But we do know that red foxes still live at the city cemetery.

Red fox facts

NAME: Red foxes are named for the most common color of their fur. Their scientific name, *Vulpes vulpes*, comes from the Latin word for "fox" or "cunning." In Spanish, they are *zorro*, which simply means "fox." They are members of the Canidae, the dog family.

SIZE: Thick fur and generous tails make red foxes look larger than they actually are. Adult red foxes stand about fifteen inches tall at the shoulder and stretch three-and-a-half feet long, nose to tail. (Nearly half that length is tail.) They tip the scales at around twelve pounds, the size of a big house cat.

COLOR: Besides rust-red, "red" foxes also come in gray, black with silver tips, and yellow marked with a dark cross of hairs over the shoulders.

VOICE: Like all dogs, red foxes bark, growl, whine, and whimper. They also make a soft cooing sound, and sometimes scream like mountain lions.

RANGE: Red foxes are the most widespread wild dogs in the world. They live throughout the northern half of the Northern Hemisphere, including most of North America.

HABITAT: A quilt-patch mix of different habitats is ideal for red foxes. In rural areas, they prefer farms, meadows, brushy places, and woods. In cities and urban areas, look for them in open spaces: cemeteries, large parks, golf courses, and airports.

In winter, red foxes don't use dens. Instead, they sleep wherever they get tired. With their tail curled around them just like a blanket, red foxes can survive temperatures far below freezing. After they mate, they dig a den or "remodel" an abandoned den to raise their family.

DIET: Like their coyote cousins, red foxes are omnivores—they eat whatever is easy to find, including mice, voles, rabbits, ground squirrels, gophers, and birds and bird eggs. They also dine on frogs, snakes, insects, raspberries, strawberries, cherries, apples, acorns, and corn. Along the seashore, red foxes eat crabs and other seafood. In urban areas, they devour pet food, food scrounged from trash cans, and garden fruits and vegetables. Being omnivorous helps red foxes survive in an urban habitat, where food is abundant but variable.

BEHAVIOR: Night creatures, red foxes' day begins at dusk. Keen senses of hearing and smell allow them to hunt in darkness. During the day they rest, taking short naps and waking frequently to see what is happening. In urban areas, red foxes hunt during the day more often, perhaps because there are fewer predators during the day than at night.

Red foxes pair up and mate from December through March. The babies are born in spring; litters average four to six kits. The kits are born with their eyes closed, and stay in the den for their first month.

Their mother nurses them for their first four or five weeks. After that, the kits eat solid food. They are full-grown by fall.

At the end of their first summer, the kits leave in search of their own territory. Depending on the availability of suitable habitat and the number of red foxes around, they may roam as far as a hundred miles from their birthplace. Red fox territories range in size from one-third of a square mile to eight square miles. The kits are ready to mate their first winter.

Red foxes are social animals. They live in pairs or family groups. Like human families, the composition of fox families varies a lot. A pair may mate for life, but if one dies, the survivor finds a new mate. A family may include several females and

their kits. Or it may be a single parent plus kits. Sometimes female kits from the previous year stay with their parents and help raise the next year's babies.

A family often uses the same den year after year to rear kits.

LIFESPAN: Wild red foxes live two to three years on average. (In captivity, however, they can survive as long as twelve years.) Predators such as hawks and owls, coyotes, wolves, domestic dogs and cats, and rattlesnakes kill them, as do humans.

Photographer's story

Wildlife photographer Wendy Shattil discovered the fox family living in the cemetery one spring afternoon when she was visiting her grandmother's grave. She returned nearly every day for the next six weeks to photograph the family.

BEING A PHOTOGRAPHER: Wildlife photography is hard work. A normal work day for Wendy and her partner, photographer Bob Rozinski, is twelve or fourteen hours. To photograph the foxes, Wendy spent several hours in her truck at the cemetery each day, watching and shooting pictures. In over a hundred hours of observation, she shot more than 1,600 photos.

EDUCATION: Wendy studied photography in college. But most of her wildlife photography knowledge, she says, was gained in the outdoors behind a camera.

SPECIAL SKILLS: Being a wildlife photographer is challenging. It means being up when animals are—early morning and late evening. It means being willing to sit still for hours at a time, even in nasty weather. It means practicing photography a lot and having an eye for detail. It means learning about your subjects, too. Wendy reads books and magazine articles about wildlife, watches television shows, and talks to experts. And being a wildlife photographer means respecting the wildlife, says Wendy. Always keep your distance. Use telephoto lenses that bring

the subject close, but not the photographer. Wendy often photographs from her truck, using it as a "blind," to keep the animals from getting used to her presence.

Most importantly, says Wendy, look around you. Although Wendy and Bob's work has taken them to exotic places, from the frozen North to tropical jungles, many of Wendy's favorite wildlife photographs have been shot near their city home.

The photos in this book were shot with a Canon camera, using an 840-mm lens mounted on a homemade window mount.